STORIES FR

Stories from

These stories come from many different countries, and are about very different people – an African-American teenager in the USA; a sad and silent wife in Malaysia, a young man in a Nigerian cyber café. But one thing is always the same. What makes them happy, or sad, or afraid is the same for all of us. A young mother in Nigeria finding a terrifying answer to a mystery makes us afraid too. The kindness of a street fruit-seller in Jamaica makes us happy. A loving wife in New Zealand making the last present for her sick husband makes us sad. And the story of the vet and Granny's cow in South Africa will surely make anyone smile...

BOOKWORMS WORLD STORIES

English has become an international language, and is used on every continent, in many varieties, for all kinds of purposes. *Bookworms World Stories* are the latest addition to the Oxford Bookworms Library. Their aim is to bring the best of the world's stories to the English language learner, and to celebrate the use of English for storytelling all around the world.

Jennifer Bassett
Series Editor

NOTE ON THE STORIES

The eight stories in this book were selected
from the winning stories in the 2004, 2005, and 2006
Commonwealth Short Story Competitions.

Regional winner (Southern Africa) 2004:
Tod Collins (South Africa) for
'The Festive Season in a Part of Africa'

Winners of Highly Commended stories 2004:
Sefi Atta (Nigeria) for 'The Photograph'
Janet Tay Hui Ching (Malaysia) for 'Callus'
Adrienne M. Frater (New Zealand) for 'Leonard'
Erica N. Robinson (Jamaica) for 'The House'

Winners of Highly Commended stories 2005:
Anthony C. Diala for (Nigeria) for 'The Strange Child'
Suchitra Karthik Kumar (India) for 'Chinna and Muthu'

Winner of Highly Commended stories 2006:
Folakemi Emem-Akpan (Nigeria) for 'The Deceivers'

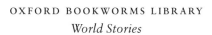

OXFORD BOOKWORMS LIBRARY

World Stories

Stories from the Heart

Stories from Around the World

Stage 2 (700 headwords)

Series Editor: Jennifer Bassett
Founder Editor: Tricia Hedge
Activities Editors: Jennifer Bassett and Christine Lindop

NOTES ON THE ILLUSTRATORS

KWAME NYONG'O (illustrations on pages 3, 9, 19, 28, 38) was born in Chicago, USA, and now lives in Nairobi in Kenya. He has been a freelance artist for many years, working in book illustration, animation, and character design. These were his first illustrations for a book for English language learners.

MESHACK ASARE (illustrations on pages 14, 15, 23, 25) was born in Ghana in 1945. He studied Art, and later, Social Anthropology, and was a teacher for many years. He is now a very well-known writer and illustrator of children's books. His books have won numerous awards, including Noma and UNESCO awards, and have been published in many countries.

CHANDRAMOHAN KULKARNI (illustrations on pages 34, 35) was born in 1956 in Pune, Maharashtra, India. He has been a freelance artist for many years, working in book illustration and cover design. He has done almost 5,000 cover designs, and illustrates contemporary literature in Marathi, a local Indian language. His work is shown in exhibitions throughout India.

RETOLD BY JENNIFER BASSETT

Stories from the Heart
Stories from Around the World

OXFORD UNIVERSITY PRESS

OXFORD
UNIVERSITY PRESS

Great Clarendon Street, Oxford, OX2 6DP, United Kingdom

Oxford University Press is a department of the University of Oxford.
It furthers the University's objective of excellence in research, scholarship,
and education by publishing worldwide. Oxford is a registered trade
mark of Oxford University Press in the UK and in certain other countries

This simplified edition © Oxford University Press 2018

The moral rights of the author have been asserted

First published in Oxford Bookworms 2018

10 9 8 7 6 5 4 3 2 1

ISBN: 978 0 19 464279 4

A complete recording of this Bookworms edition of
Stories from the Heart: Stories from Around the World is available.

Printed in China

Word count (main text): 6,361

For more information on the Oxford Bookworms Library,
visit www.oup.com/elt/gradedreaders

ACKNOWLEDGEMENTS

Cover illustration by: Lila Kalogeri/Advocate Art

Other illustrations by: Meshack Asare pp.14, 15, 23, 25;
Chandramohan Kulkarni pp.34, 35; Kwame Nyong'o pp.3, 9, 19, 28, 38

Copyright of original texts:
The Photograph original text © Sefi Atta 2004
Callus original text © Janet Tay Hui Ching 2003
The Festive Season in a Part of Africa original text © Tod Collins 2004
The Strange Child © Anthony C. Diala 2005
The Deceivers © Folakemi Emem-Akpan 2006
Leonard original text © Adrienne M Frater 2004
Chinna and Muthu © Suchitra Karthik Kumar 2005
The House original text © Erica N Robinson 2004
This simplified edition © Oxford University Press 2018

The stories are selected from the winning entries of the Commonwealth
Short Story Competition administered by the Commonwealth Broadcasting
Association and funded by the Commonwealth Foundation.

The publishers are grateful to the following for permission to adapt and simplify copyright texts:
Sefi Atta for *The Photograph*; Janet Tay Hui Ching for *Callus*; Tod Collins for *The Festive Season
in a Part of Africa*; Anthony C. Diala for *The Strange Child*; Folakemi Emem-Akpan for *The Deceivers*;
Adrienne M Frater for *Leonard*; Suchitra Karthik Kumar for *Chinna and Muthu*;
Erica N Robinson for *The House*

CONTENTS

NOTE ON THE LANGUAGE

There are many varieties of English spoken in the world, and the characters in these stories sometimes use non-standard forms (for example, leaving out auxiliary verbs such as *do*, or *am*, *are*, *is*). This is how the authors of the original stories represented the spoken language that their characters would actually use in real life.

There are also words that are usually only found in a particular variety of English (for example, *kraal* in South African English and *dutty* in Jamaican English). In some stories there are a few words from other languages (for example, *samfoo* from Cantonese and *Aiyya* from Hindi). All these words are either explained in the stories or in the glossary on page 41.

The Photograph

SEFI ATTA

~

A story from Nigeria, retold by Jennifer Bassett

In today's world there are photographs everywhere – web pages on the internet, magazines full of fashion and film stars, newspapers full of photos of war and sport, places and people from other lands.

They say a picture is worth a thousand words, and maybe it is, but what is the picture telling us? Sometimes we only see what we want to see...

Make a picture in your mind: a girl with thin cheeks and tired eyes. Her arms and legs are as thin as sticks; she is only skin and bone. Clouds of dust circle above her head as the food trucks drive away. Their wheels leave marks on the dry ground, and soon only the marks show that the food trucks came to the village, and left.

The sun is at its hottest; the African sky is unending and cruel. Even the white men with cameras, busily taking photographs of the usual fighting over the food, are now getting ready to leave. They pack away their cameras, jump into their cars, and drive quickly away to cool, modern hotels in a city miles away. They are photojournalists.

One of them, sun-burned and hot, dressed in a shirt and jeans, kneels down on the dusty ground to take some photographs of the girl before he leaves. In the pocket of his shirt is a protein bar, soft from the sun, uneaten, untouched, forgotten.

He doesn't stop to think about the uneaten bar in his pocket and the starving girl. He is only one man. What can one man do in a world where life is cruel, and governments cannot or will not help their people? And who wants to stay in a place like this, with its dirt and its terrible smells, if they can drive away from it?

The girl caught the photographer's eye. She was in the middle of a group of boys, fighting just as strongly as they were, when the food trucks arrived. But she was pushed down and fell under the boys' feet. The boys stepped all over her, and when she could move again, the bags of rice were all gone. She stayed there, red-eyed, moving her fingers slowly over the dusty ground.

～

The journalist takes his last photo, returns to America with his bag full of films. One of his photographs of the girl sells and is placed on the front cover of a news magazine.

'You've caught the face of hunger in Africa,' the news editor tells him.

The girl stayed there, red-eyed, moving her fingers slowly over the dusty ground.

He wants to tell the editor that this photograph is just one face, in one village, in a country full of hungry faces. But he does not say it. The photograph is good for him. More people admire his work and want to buy his photographs for their magazines and newspapers.

The photograph is in most news stores by the end of the month, even in those bookstores where people go only to read the magazines and not to buy. They look at the face of the African girl, and quickly turn away to enjoy the rest of their shopping trip.

But the girl's picture stays in their minds.

A teenager has just finished looking at the clothes in *Vogue*, an expensive fashion magazine. She sees the photograph under the heading STARVING AFRICA. Her parents are from Africa. She herself was born and schooled in America, watching American TV, American films, and has never travelled out of America. She is uncomfortable with photographs like these. She remembers her classmates in school, who joke about starving Africans. She isn't African in *that* kind of way, but she isn't truly American either.

When she was younger, Cinderella, Snow White, and all the other girls and princesses in the Disney films didn't look like her. When she was older and became interested in fashion, the models on the magazine covers didn't look like her either. Then the magazines found out that Africa had beautiful women.

A Nigerian model is in the latest copy of *Vogue*, dressed in blue, and thin, so thin. The teenager feels the fat at the top of her legs. She wants to be thin like the model. She wants to wear jeans that are like a second skin. She wants a photograph of herself with cool, unsmiling eyes like the Nigerian model. She is careful about what she eats, and if she eats too much, she puts her finger down her throat to make herself sick.

Why does our world have people who starve, and people who decide to starve themselves? It doesn't matter why. The hunger inside this teenager is real. So she stares at the girl in the photograph, does not think about the dry dusty hungry land behind her, and admires her cheek bones.

Leonard

ADRIENNE M. FRATER

~

A story from New Zealand, retold by Jennifer Bassett

*Women often knit gifts for their families.
Wives knit socks or scarves for their husbands;
grandmothers knit little jackets for their
children's babies.*

*Buying a gift is quick and easy, but making
a gift with your own hands takes longer. And
if, like Leonard's wife, your hands are old and
stiff and crooked with arthritis, perhaps
knitting is not the best thing to do...*

I'll knit him a scarf. Yes. I'll knit him a scarf the same
colour as his eyes.

I'll wait until my niece takes me shopping. 'I want to
buy some wool,' I tell her. 'I want to knit Leonard a scarf.'

'But you don't knit,' she says. She looks at my crooked
hands and quickly looks away again. 'And Leonard
doesn't go out any more.'

But Petra takes me to the wool shop anyway.

'I want to buy some blue wool,' I say to the woman
in the shop. 'The colour of my husband's eyes.' I touch
a ball of blue wool that feels as soft as a bird's feathers.

'Isn't this a little too fine?' asks the woman in the shop.

'No, it's just right.'

~

Later, tired after my shopping, I lie back in my armchair and have a little sleep.

When the car stops outside, I am still half asleep, and in my mind I see a younger Leonard standing at the door. His back is as straight as a piece of wood, and his blue eyes smile.

'Is anyone home?' Dan calls.

I wake with a jump.

'Here we are, Mr Phipps,' Dan says to Leonard. Holding Leonard's arm, Dan walks him into the house.

'Thank you, Dan.' I take off Leonard's coat and push some hair away from his eyes.

We eat dinner in a silence that aches. I drink red wine and Leonard eats with a spoon. Then, after I've washed him and put him to bed, I sit down to knit.

The needles are silver. The needles are cold. I take the paper cover off the wool, find one end of it, and try again and again to make the first stitch. I am listening to music by Beethoven, and it is nearly halfway through before I have finished the first row of stitches. My fingers hurt, and they won't do what I tell them. But I have begun.

~

Leonard and I met at a concert in Auckland. He was tall, with blond hair then. I can still see him walking towards my seat. He took off the soft blue scarf that was the same colour as his eyes, and my heart gave a little jump. We talked over supper, and I found out where he lived and what he did.

'I'm an eye doctor,' he said, 'just beginning. No money, but I never miss concerts.'

I made our first date while we were walking out of the concert building. In those days men always did the asking, not girls. I don't know if Leonard was surprised at my asking him or not. He never said anything.

～

On the days when Leonard goes to the day-care centre, I knit. I plan to finish the scarf for our fifty-third wedding anniversary. The scarf is almost finished, and when I hold it to the light, diamonds shine through. I shake the wool, drop a stitch, try to find it again. Was I more in love with Leonard than he was with me? I have so many questions … and I cannot ask any of them now.

'It's finished,' I tell my niece, putting the scarf round my neck.

'It looks good,' she said, 'if you don't look too closely. Is it a gift?'

'Yes. My last.'

On the morning of our anniversary I kiss Leonard and give him the scarf. I know he will not speak, but while I am putting the scarf round his neck, I find that I am still hoping.

*On the morning of our anniversary I kiss Leonard
and give him the scarf.*

The scarf is as crooked as my fingers. It's full of holes – long thin holes, little round holes. Leonard puts his hand up and touches the wool, and for one short moment, his eyes come alive again.

'Yes,' he wants to tell me. 'Yes,' he wants to say.

'The scarf is soft.

      The scarf is blue.

         The scarf is us.'

The Strange Child

ANTHONY C. DIALA

~

A story from Nigeria, retold by Jennifer Bassett

Before young people get married, they usually meet each other's families – mother, father, brothers, sisters. And everybody comes to the wedding, to celebrate the joining of two families.

Linda has been married to Emeka for nearly three years, but she has never met his family. She is unhappy about this, and decides to change things. But sometimes it is better not to ask questions...

Linda lay in bed, turning from side to side. She could not sleep. There was a question in her mind that was as old as her marriage – a question that did not go away, a question that had no answer. Something about her husband puzzled her, but she could not decide what it was. She stared for a long time at the ceiling. And then, at last, Linda woke her husband.

Emeka turned to look at her. His eyes were sleepy.

'What is it?' he said, staring at his wife.

'My love, I have been your wife for almost three years. During this time, how often have I asked to meet your family? And every time you say no. I know nothing about your past life, or your family, and I cannot stay married to a man who is a mystery. So, I have decided. If you still won't take me to your village, I shall go alone with our son this weekend. I must meet your family.'

Emeka stared at the wall. Linda wanted to win this long battle between them. He could hear it in her voice. The fight was over. He could not stop her, and he had nothing more to say.

'Do what you want,' he said. 'I don't know why you want to see my family. They will never welcome you. They don't want to see me. They disowned me years ago – I've told you that many times. I don't ever want to see them again.'

He turned on his side and went back to sleep.

Three days later, Linda travelled to Emeka's village with her two-year-old son. She drove carefully through the narrow roads in her small sports car. The countryside was beautiful, she thought, with its hills and its thick green forests. But the houses were poor and not at all beautiful.

Near the end of the journey she began to feel excited. She stopped to ask the way, then at last she arrived at a small house, which looked old and uncared for.

In the house were a grey-haired old man and a young man, who was Emeka's brother. 'The house is empty today,' the old man explained, 'because Saturday is the village market day.' He offered Linda kola nut and a calabash of water; these were the usual things offered to a visitor in the countryside.

Linda was pleased and thankful for this welcome. She then told her story, beginning from the day when she met her husband at a gas station.

The old man and Emeka's brother looked more and more puzzled. When Linda finished her story, she showed them her marriage certificate and pictures of her husband.

'Please,' she said, 'please, please forgive him.'

The old man stared silently at the floor for a long time. Emeka's brother moved uncomfortably in his seat.

Linda held her son's hand tightly and watched the two men worriedly. 'What are they thinking about?' she thought. 'Will they welcome me to the family?'

After some time, the old man stood up.

'Come, my daughter,' he said. 'I am Emeka's father, so I cannot lie to you. Follow me please.'

The old man took her outside the house, to the edge of the yard. He stopped under a huge mango tree. He pointed to the ground under the tree.

'Emeka is buried there,' he said quietly. 'He died in a car crash, exactly three years ago. He is my son and I loved him very much. We never disowned him.'

Linda stood as still as a stone. Her mind stopped working; she saw and heard nothing.

The old man stopped under a huge mango tree.
He pointed to the ground under the tree.

Emeka's father looked unhappily at the little boy standing beside her. He looked exactly the same as Emeka at that age. The old man was filled with worry. What will happen, he thought, to this strange, strange child?

The House

ERICA N. ROBINSON

~

A story from Jamaica, retold by Jennifer Bassett

Sometimes people's lives go terribly wrong – maybe their marriage breaks down, they lose their job, their house, their friends; they have to live on the street, they drink too much, they don't wash...

Who will give a man like that a second chance? Only a very special kind of person – like Nan, a fruit-seller on the streets of Kingston...

Sonny had a new plan, but he did not know if Nan would agree to it.

He and Jake were building a house, which was big enough for two families. And one day they decided between them that Sonny's ex-wife Tanya and his children should have it.

'Nan,' Sonny said to her quietly, 'I going to let Tanya and the children live in the house.'

'What!' shouted Nan. 'Why?'

'It is good for the children,' said Sonny. 'They will be off the streets, and the boys won't have to hustle like me.'

'But what about me and you? Where we going to live?'

'We will try and build another one,' Sonny said.

Lord, he thought, is she going to leave me now? Maybe this is too much for her. I love her. I hope she understands what I'm trying to do.

'So...' Nan said slowly. 'You tell Tanya already?'

'I said something about it.' Sonny looked away from Nan's eyes. 'She agrees because it would be good for the children. I don't want my daughters living and dying like dogs on the streets of Kingston, and I don't want my boys carrying guns and selling drugs. I want them to have a place to live, Nan, a place where they can study their books and have a better life.'

'It is a hard thing you ask, Sonny,' Nan said quietly.

~

Sonny was a good man, and Nan trusted him. But she could not understand why he still cared about his ex-wife Tanya. Why can't he have a clean break with this woman, she thought. Tanya ruined his life – she went with other men and she kicked him out on the street. And then she sold all his things.

Nan remembered the day when she first met Sonny – a day that changed her life. He was just a street man, a drunkard, and so dirty. There was hunger in his face, in his eyes, even in the way he walked. She watched him for a while, then called out to him.

'Old man, come here. You hungry?'

'Yes, Ma'am.'

What kind of a street man was this, she thought. Nobody ever called her Ma'am. That wasn't a word people said to women who sold fruit on street corners. They usually called out 'old girl', or something worse like 'dutty sketel'. It felt good, to be called Ma'am.

She took some of her fruit and gave it to him.

'Thank you, Miss,' he said. 'I'm very grateful.'

He came by every day after that, and every day she gave him some fruit. Then one day she took him to the church on Harbour Street, which helped street people with their drink problems. They agreed to help him and took him in.

~

Two months later a clean, tidy man in a light brown suit stopped by her stall and said, 'How are you, Madam?' He gave a big smile, showing his white teeth. 'Here's something for you,' he said, and held out two 1,000 dollar bills.

'Thank you,' Nan said, 'but why you giving me so much money?'

'You helped me when I needed someone,' he said quietly. 'You brought me back to life.'

Nan stared at him, not understanding.

'I was that old drunkard on the streets,' he explained, 'and you gave me food every day.'

'What!' said Nan. 'I happy to see that you alright now.'

*Sonny came by every day after that, and every day
Nan gave him some fruit.*

'Yes, thanks to you. I now have a job with the town council, you know. I drive the garbage truck.'

Nan smiled happily. She went on smiling for the next year and a half. She felt young again, and full of hope. At last she could forget the sad years when she was sixteen, with a baby, and no chance to go to school and get a better life for herself. She and Sonny started living together, and now they were planning to get married and have a home of their own. She decided to give Sonny this one thing, and to give it freely, because she trusted him.

'Okay, go on,' she said to Sonny, 'let them live in the house, and we will work together to build our own.'

Sonny put his long arms around Nan's comfortable body and pulled her close. He understood what she was saying – that she trusted him, that she was strong enough to wait.

He put his mouth close to her ear and whispered 'Thank you'.

The Deceivers

FOLAKEMI EMEM-AKPAN

~

A story from Nigeria, retold by Jennifer Bassett

Many people these days use computers to talk to people all over the world. They meet in chat rooms, and talk by typing in questions and answers. They often don't use their own names, and never see the person's face or hear their voice.

Gbenga is in a cyber café, sitting in front of a computer, ready to log in to the Yahoo chat room and talk to his new friend...

Gbenga hit the enter key on the computer keyboard, and waited for Yahoo to accept his login. He moved his long legs around under the desk, trying to get comfortable. This afternoon he was not Gbenga from Nigeria; he was Celia, a girl from ... somewhere in the US. The computer didn't need to know where.

While Gbenga waited, he looked around the cyber café. Just the usual crowd – people looking for jobs, school students not in school, a few workers without the internet in their offices.

Soon, the login was done. Excitedly, Gbenga clicked on mervyn360@yahoo.com. He already knew Mervyn from the last time he was online as Celia. They chatted for a while and got friendly, so they made a date to chat again today. Now, if he played the game well…

'Hi, Mervyn. Are you there?' he typed hurriedly, and hit the enter key.

The reply came almost immediately. 'Yeah. Been waiting for you.'

'Sorry I'm late. I just got back from school. Man, it was hard work.'

'School?' came the reply.

'Yes. School.'

'You go to night school?'

'I mean…' And then Gbenga remembered that it was early morning in the States, and he – Celia – was living in the States. 'I'm studying for my exams and take an hour of extra lessons each morning.'

'Oh, didn't know that. So where do you live?

'Kentucky.' Gbenga typed quickly. He was ready for that question.

'Where in Kentucky?'

'Louisville. Want to come for a visit?'

'That would be cool. It's not far from here. I live in Frankfort.'

'Whoa, just around the corner!' Now to more important things, Gbenga thought.

'You're not a student, are you?' he typed.

'No. I work with my father. He's an architect.'

Gbenga typed hurriedly, and hit the enter key.
The reply came almost immediately.

'You're an architect too?' typed Gbenga.

'Yep. You don't like architects?'

'I do ... I do, I mean ...' Gbenga started thinking hard. Here was Mervyn, American, with money, and believing he was Celia. What could he do? How could he get some dollars out of Mervyn? He couldn't think of an easy answer. He decided to go on playing with Mervyn, getting friendly. And then he would ask his friends to help him make a good plan.

'You guys have a big architects' company?' Gbenga typed.

'Sure. Now don't do all the asking. I've got questions of my own. You live alone?'

'Yes.'

'Maybe I'll come for that visit. If you invite me...'

'Later.'

'That doesn't sound very welcoming!'

'Sorry, didn't mean to sound like that. By the way, what's your surname?'

The reply did not come fast, so Gbenga sat back in his seat to rest a while.

A young guy sitting opposite him in the café looked up at him. A dirty pair of glasses was pushed far down on his fat nose. Not a pretty face, Gbenga decided.

'Excuse me,' said the young guy.

'Yeah?' Gbenga said.

'Can you please spell Prescott?' the guy asked.

'As in …?'

'Prescott as in a name. I'm chatting with some babe and she needs me to tell her my surname.'

A sudden surprise ran through Gbenga, but he spelt the name aloud for the guy.

'Thanks. Do you …'

Gbenga turned away quickly. His screen was flashing, *NEW MESSAGE RECEIVED*. It was Mervyn's reply.

'Prescott, my surname is Prescott,' appeared on Gbenga's computer screen.

Gbenga's surprise changed immediately into a sudden anger. He looked at the guy with dirty glasses.

'Hey, what login name are you using?'

'That's not your business!'

Gbenga stood up, all six foot of him. 'What login name are you using?' he said angrily.

'Mervyn360@yahoo.com. You got a problem with that?'

Callus

JANET TAY HUI CHING

~

A story from Malaysia, retold by Jennifer Bassett

Some people don't find it easy to talk about their feelings. If they have never talked about them, it can be hard to begin. And year after year, it gets harder and harder – just like a callus on the skin.

A wife watches while her husband packs his suitcase. A great change is coming into their lives, but maybe it is easier to talk about the suitcase...

She watched him pack his clothes and his wedding suit into his old suitcase. She could smell his cologne. When did he last wear cologne? Ah, at their wedding. It smelt strange then too. She never wore perfume. What use was perfume to a working woman like her? And married women who wear perfume are looking for lovers, trying to catch other men. That's what people say. She already had a good, hardworking husband with a shop of his own. What more can a woman want?

She began to feel better now, thinking about her good luck.

Lost in her thoughts, she jumped at the sound of the

suitcase shutting. His eyes went slowly round the room, looking for – what? She looked up at him.

'I put out all the clothes that you need,' she said. 'And you can't get any more in. It's a small suitcase.'

He looked at her for a moment. A Chinese girl like any other Chinese girl – small eyes, flat nose, smooth pale skin, and long straight hair, now pinned up tidily, in the way of married Chinese ladies. She wore her usual light blue samfoo. No, she was not a beauty, he thought, but she was a hard worker. His family was right when they said to him, 'She will make a very good wife, work hard for you, give you many sons.'

And it was true. He never had to complain about her, not once, from the day they married and moved into their new home, with his future in the same suitcase. Her face was the same now as it was then, neither soft nor hard, never showing what she felt or needed. He didn't know what she needed. And he never asked.

'It's a good suitcase. It's lasted a long time,' he said.

'Yes, I suppose. But it's still small.'

She got up from the bed and shook the pillows. They needed washing, she thought. Yes, wash it away, the dust and dirt of yesterday. Their past married life together. In the future nothing would ever be the same again.

'It's enough,' he said. 'I don't have so many things to put in it.' He put the suitcase on the floor, ready to go.

She looked at him, still smelling his cologne. Maybe it

Her face never showed what she felt or needed. He didn't know what she needed. And he never asked.

was the cologne that was making her feel afraid. She had to talk to him, tell him about her feelings. But she was a hard-working Chinese woman … and hard-working Chinese women must not have feelings.

'Is she waiting for you there?' she asked slowly.

'You mean the hotel?'

'Yes. I suppose the ceremony starts soon?'

She picked up one of the pillows and took off its cover. Yes, it needed washing. She wanted to get hold of him and shake him, scream and shout, and fall on her knees in front of him, crying 'No, no, please stay, don't go. I'll be a better wife. I'll work harder. I'll work as hard as two wives.' But she just stood there, saying nothing, doing nothing, her face showing nothing.

'I suppose,' he said.

'You'll be back in two days?'

He didn't want to talk about her feelings. She never did before. But then it wasn't every day that your husband brought home a new wife. A younger wife. Only nineteen. And beautiful because she was young and happy, and had big dark brown eyes – bright eyes. He only saw her once before he decided, but he remembered her eyes. It would be good to add her to the family, he thought. Now he would have two hard-working wives, one stronger than the other, but the young one would be like a new flower in the house. He picked up his suitcase.

'Yes, perhaps sooner. I don't know,' he said.

'I'll take care of the shop,' she said. 'When you come back … with her … I'll have some jobs for her to do.'

She sat on the bed again, suddenly feeling tired and old. He didn't understand. No one understood. She couldn't ask him not to go. People would say that she was wrong even to ask him.

'Of course,' he said. He was pleased that she thought of business. Business was important. He had many mouths to feed. He opened the door and turned to her.

'Today is a great day for our family. Not everyone is rich enough to have two wives. And there will be more sons to continue the family name.' He smiled at her.

'Yes. Not everyone … Husband?' She looked up at him, waiting, hoping.

'I have to go now. I'm late.' He did not want her to say anything. He never asked questions about her feelings because he was afraid of the answers. It was easier to pretend that she was happy all the time.

'Your suitcase. It's old. You need a new one.'

Thankfully, he turned away. No questions asked, no answers needed.

'Perhaps I will get a new one after all,' he said. He left the room and the door closed quietly behind him.

Chinna and Muthu

SUCHITRA KARTHIK KUMAR

~

A story from India, retold by Jennifer Bassett

*In some places in the world, life is hard.
When the rain does not fall, your fields
turn brown and your cattle die. Soon you
will die too. You have to do something, and
surely the old ways are best.*

*But Chinna is just a young boy, a child.
He doesn't know the old ways, he doesn't
know what is best. Or does he?*

Thwack! For a second the big black bird did not move, then it fell softly to the ground.

'Chinna, you're the best!'

The catapult dropped out of little Chinna's hands. He looked at the dead black bird on the ground, and tried not to cry. He did not hear his friends, calling and laughing and shouting how clever he was.

~

That year the sun burned down on the village. The land was brown and dry – and thirsty; the cattle were thirsty, the plants in the fields were thirsty, people were thirsty. Water was drying up. The Rain Gods were angry, and they needed a sacrifice.

Chinna was the only son of Nachiappa Gounder, the village chief, and the sacrifice would happen in the chief's house. The sacrifice of a goat.

The men brought the goat in when Chinna was having lunch. Chinna stared at it as it went out into the back yard, its little feet dancing on the hard floor, like a dancer's shoes. It had unusually big eyes for a goat.

Chinna lay awake, his eyes wide open. It was long past midnight, and the night air was hot and still. He could not sleep, so he jumped up and went out into the yard. He picked up a stone and threw it carelessly into the old cattle-shed. Almost immediately, there was a noise. Chinna looked inside. The little goat was awake, and was walking up and down, up and down.

'Hold still, hold still.' Chinna put his arms around the goat. It felt soft and warm, and had a wonderfully sweet smell of milk and hay. It made a little noise, and Chinna smiled.

'My name is Chinna, but you don't have a name, no? Hmm … Let's think. Muthu? Muthu was my dog.'

The boy and the goat sat quietly. Chinna told Muthu everything about his life, and then he looked up at the moon in the sky. Tomorrow it would be full. Like a great ball of yellow gold.

Tomorrow.

Chinna felt cold.

The next morning the house was full of noise and people running, shouting, laughing. The women gave Chinna a bath, then took him to the yard. The drums were already beating loudly; everything was ready for the sacrifice.

'Bring in the goat,' the priest called.

Chinna hid behind one of the women.

A man came running into the yard. 'Aiyya! The goat is missing!'

The drums stopped. Everything was suddenly quiet. Then everybody began to cry out at the same time.

'The Gods are angry with us!'

'We will die, we will all die!'

'Not one drop of rain will touch our land!'

'QUIET!'

It was Chinna's father. 'There is no need to be afraid. We will break a pumpkin for the Gods. It is a present from our land, from our own fields. The Gods will surely accept this from us.'

For a few moments there was a lot of talk and noise. There was also one very quiet conversation between Nachiappa Gounder and the priest, during which there was a promise of two fields of good land. After this conversation, the priest called out:

'Be quiet! Gounder Aiyya knows what is good for all of us. Why have the drums stopped? Start the singing!'

The drums and the singing got louder and louder. The men brought in a large pumpkin and gave it to the chief.

'There is no need to be afraid,' Nachiappa Gounder said.
'We will break a pumpkin for the Gods.'

Before Nachiappa Gounder put the pumpkin down on the table of sacrifice, he stopped and looked at Chinna.

Chinna's ears felt burning hot. He stared back at his father's face. The sun was in his eyes, and he couldn't see clearly. Was that a smile, or an angry stare?

That night, the boy and the goat sat under Chinna's favourite tree. Chinna stared at the river, while Muthu pushed her nose into Chinna's hand, looking for food. Chinna was thinking hard. Did his father know about this secret place too? Chinna smiled, and threw a stone, trying to make it jump over the water. The stone sank, leaving behind a ripple on the water, and another ... then another ...

Then Chinna felt it on his arm and looked up. A drop. And another.

The skies opened, and fell down on the only two sleepless things in the village that night. Wonderful, warm, kindly, and heavy.

Rain.

The Festive Season in a Part of Africa

TOD COLLINS

~

A story from South Africa, retold by Jennifer Bassett

> *If you are a poor farmer and you only have one cow, it is important that it doesn't get sick. Because if it does, and you need to get a vet to come and see it, that can be very expensive.*
>
> *But if you are afraid that your cow will die, then you must send for the vet – even if it is the festive season and Christmas was only two days ago...*

Two days after Christmas a Zulu woman and her schoolboy son sat waiting for me to finish my morning's clinic in Ondini. She wanted me to visit her old mother's cow, which had a calf waiting to be born. But for two days now the calf would not come out, and the poor cow was getting very tired. 'We have heard that you are a good vet,' the woman said to me.

So off we went. The schoolboy in the front of my pick-up, to show me the way, and the woman and my assistant Mbambo in the back. An hour of driving on bad roads full of holes and after that on dirt tracks. Then we stopped at an old empty kraal.

'Where's the cow?' I asked the boy.

'We walk a bit,' he said.

So we took my vet's black bags and we walked. Past other kraals with their fields and their fruit trees, and many of them with huts not lived in and falling down. We walked over rocks and by the side of rivers and after about forty-five minutes we came to a lonely kraal. There were three white huts, a clean tidy yard, and there under the fruit trees was the poor old cow, looking very, very tired.

They brought out two nice wooden chairs with colourful seats from the middle hut. I put my black bags on them, but first, I said hello in the proper Zulu way to Granny, who owned the cow. 'Inkosikazi' I called her. She was a very small woman, but she was the head of her family in the kraal.

Then I looked at the cow and found that the calf was still alive, and very, very big. So, with Mbambo helping me, I put the cow to sleep and did a caesarean.

When I finished, there was a crowd of about fifty people watching – men standing, older women sitting on the ground, children sitting in the fruit trees. Now the bullcalf was trying to stand on his feet, and shaking his head from side to side.

Someone brought a chair for Granny to sit on.

'We must talk about money. Is business now,'
Granny called out so everyone could hear.

'We must talk about money. Is business now,' she called out so everyone could hear.

'Well,' I said, 'you nearly had a dead cow and a dead calf, but I came and got the calf out, and so now they are both alive, not so?'

She agreed, and fifty other people agreed too.

'And I drove all the way from Ondini in my pick-up which is a thirsty car – as thirsty as an old man drinking beer on a Sunday.'

Smiles and laughter.

'And if you take good care of this calf and he grows into a strong young bull, when he is a year old, at the market in Ondini, they will pay you 1,500 rands for him. Not so?'

'Yes.' The old men in the crowd nodded their heads.

'And the cow ... she is old and tired, and the flies are very bad this summer. But if she lives, next autumn you can sell her for over 2,500 rands.'

Loud noises of agreement from the crowd.

'So then, Inkosikazi, my work has given you about 4,000 rands that you didn't have before.'

'Yes.'

'So how about we go halves – and I take 2,000 rands?'

Much whispering between Granny and her friends.

'That's lots of money,' she said.

'Yes, it is,' I said, 'and we have just had Christmas and soon it will be New Year, and maybe the cow will die. So it is better that I don't ask for so much. You can pay me just half of that – 750 rands.'

Louder whispering and nods of agreement.

'But!' said the schoolboy, who was standing behind his grandmother, 'half of 2,000 is not 750, it is 1,000!'

'Oh-ho!' I said. 'I can see you are a clever young man. I made a mistake, but if I said 750, then I shall still say 750 and not change it.'

Well, what a noise there was after that! Everybody was smiling and happy. Granny pulled out a great big handful of 200 rand notes, and she gave four of them to me, with her other hand open upwards next to the giving hand, in the proper Zulu way.

I took the money from her with my two open hands side by side, in the proper Zulu way, counted the notes and said, 'Inkosikazi, you have given me too much.'

She stood up and said, 'Keep the 50, it is for your assistant Mbambo.'

Man, the season of goodwill is amazing.

Then we walked back for an hour, mostly uphill, with a long line of helpers carrying my bags. We stopped sometimes to eat the sweet wild fruit that grows around most of the old kraals in this part of Africa ...

... in the festive season.

GLOSSARY

admire to think that something or somebody is very good

Aiyya *(Indian)* 'master', a man who is the boss

amazing very surprising

anniversary a day exactly one year (or more) after a special event

architect a person whose job is to design and plan buildings

arthritis a disease which causes pain in the joints of the body

assistant a person who helps another person in their work

bury to put a dead body into the ground

caesarean cutting the mother's body to take out a baby

calabash a bottle made from the dried shell of a large fruit

calf (**bullcalf**) a baby cow (a male calf)

callus a place of hard thick skin on a hand or foot

catapult a stick with a rubber band, used for shooting stones

cattle cows that are kept for their milk or meat

ceremony a formal public event (e.g. a wedding)

certificate an important piece of paper that shows something
   is true

chat friendly 'talking' (by typing, not speaking) on the internet

chief the leader or boss of a group of people

cologne a kind of light perfume

complain to say you don't like or are unhappy about something

concert a public performance of music

cool *(informal)* saying 'cool' shows you admire or like something

council a group of people who make rules for a town, city, etc.

countryside land that is away from towns and cities

crooked not straight

cruel very unkind

cyber café a café with computers where you can send emails, etc.

date a meeting with a boy/girlfriend or a possible boy/girlfriend

date (make a) to arrange a meeting with a girl/boyfriend

deceiver a person who makes somebody believe something untrue

diamond a very expensive, hard stone that looks like clear glass

disown to say that you do not want to be connected to a person

drug a dangerous thing that people put in their bodies because it makes them feel happy, excited, different, brave, etc.

drum a musical instrument that you hit with sticks or your hands

drunkard somebody who gets drunk very often

dutty *(West Indian English)* dirty

editor a person who prepares a newspaper before it is printed

ex-wife a person's former wife

feelings something (e.g. anger, fear) that you feel inside yourself

festive connected with the days when people celebrate Christmas

flash to send out a bright light that comes and goes quickly

forgive to stop being angry with someone for a bad thing they did

garbage *(North American English)* rubbish

goodwill friendly or helpful feelings towards other people

guy *(informal)* a man

huge very, very big

hustle *(North American English)* to sell things (e.g. drugs, guns) outside the law

Inkosikazi *(Zulu)* a word for Mrs, wife, madam

joke something that you do or say to make people laugh

knit to make clothes from wool using two long sticks (needles)

kola nut the seed of the kola tree

kraal *(South African English)* a village of huts with a place for keeping animals

log in to type your password etc. to begin using a computer; **login** *(n)*

mango a large fruit, yellow inside, that grows in hot countries

mind *(n)* the part of you that thinks and remembers

model a person who wears clothes for photographs

niece the daughter of your brother or sister

online using a computer or the internet

pale with not much colour

pillow a soft thing you put your head on when you are in bed

priest a person who leads people in their religion

protein bar like a bar of chocolate, but made of fruit, nuts, etc.

pumpkin a large round vegetable with thick orange skin

puzzle to feel confused because you do not understand something

ripple a small wave on the water of a lake or pond

ruin *(v)* to do great harm or damage to something

sacrifice offering something to a god (e.g. an animal that has been killed), in order to get something more important

samfoo *(Cantonese)* jacket and trousers, worn by Chinese women

scarf a piece of material that you wear around your neck or head

shed a small simple building where you keep things or animals

sketel *(West Indian English)* a woman who has too many men friends

starving in danger of dying because you do not have food to eat

stitch *(n)* a circle of wool round a needle when you are knitting

track a rough path or road

truck a big vehicle for carrying heavy things

trust *(v)* to believe that someone is good and will not hurt you

vet a doctor for animals

yard an area next to a building, usually with a wall around it

Zulu a member of a race of black people in South Africa

ACTIVITIES

Before Reading

Before you read the stories, read the introductions at the beginning. Then use these activities to help you think about the stories. How much can you guess about them?

1 *The Photograph* (story introduction page 1). Do you agree (A) or disagree (D) with these ideas?

   1 Photographs give stronger messages than words.

   2 Photographs can lie.

   3 People understand photographs more easily than words.

2 *Leonard* (story introduction page 6). What can you guess? Choose two endings.

   Leonard's wife will knit a scarf for Leonard...

   1 which will be beautiful.   3 because she loves him.

   2 which will be full of holes.   4 because he is cold.

3 *The Strange Child* (story introduction page 11). What can you guess about this story? Choose yes (Y) or no (N).

   1 Linda will learn something terrible. Y / N

   2 This story will have a happy ending. Y / N

4 *The House* (story introduction page 16). What can you guess about Nan? Choose from these ideas. She...

is cruel   cries a lot   helps people   doesn't help people
is kind   smiles a lot   trusts people   doesn't trust people

5 *The Deceivers* (story introduction page 21). What can you guess about Gbenga? Which of these sentences are true?

1 Gbenga does not use his real name in the chat room.

2 Gbenga uses a girl's name.

3 Gbenga uses the name of a very famous person.

6 *Callus* (story introduction page 26). Do you agree (**A**) or disagree (**D**) with these ideas?

1 It is always better for people to talk about their feelings.

2 Sometimes it is better to keep silent about your feelings.

3 Women are good at talking about feelings; men are not.

7 *Chinna and Muthu* (story introduction page 31). What happens to Chinna in this story? Choose some of these ideas.

1 Chinna makes a new friend.   3 Chinna is in trouble.

2 Chinna's father is angry.   4 Chinna has a secret.

8 *The Festive Season in a Part of Africa* (story introduction page 36). How many of these things will happen?

1 The cow dies.   3 The vet is very expensive.

2 The cow has a calf.   4 The vet agrees a good price.

ACTIVITIES

After Reading

1 Match these parts of sentences about people in these eight
stories. There are three parts to each sentence. Then choose
the best linking words to join the parts together.

First parts of the sentence:
1 The African girl in the photograph is starving, ...
2 Mrs Phipps is knitting a scarf for Leonard, ...
3 Linda drives to her husband's village, ...
4 Sonny was a drunkard living on the streets, ...
5 Gbenga thinks it is clever to use a false name, ...
6 A man packs his suitcase to go to his wedding...
7 Chinna knows what happens in a sacrifice...
8 Granny in South Africa sends for the vet...

Second parts of the sentence:
9 *but / because* she wants to meet his family, ...
10 *while / after* his first wife watches him unhappily...
11 *so / because* she is afraid her cow will die, ...
12 *but / so* the girl in the bookstore in the USA admires her
cheek bones...
13 *why / but* he isn't so clever after all, ...
14 *after / and* he loves the little goat, ...
15 *which / who* has been her husband for fifty-three years, ...
16 *but / because* Nan gave him some fruit...

Third parts of the sentence:

17 *because / so* the guy opposite him is doing the same thing.

18 *and / after* does not think about dying from hunger.

19 *so / why* he takes her away and hides her in a secret place.

20 *but / because* he spoke nicely to her and called her Ma'am.

21 *but / so* now he does not remember her name.

22 *because / but* the calf is born alive and all is well.

23 *so / and* tries to find the words to stop him going.

24 *so / but* she learns a terrible secret about her husband.

2 **How did you feel about the people in these stories? Use the list of names and the table below to make sentences about them. Use as many words as you like to finish the sentences.**

1 *The Photograph*: the photographer / the American girl

2 *Leonard*: Leonard / Leonard's wife

3 *The Strange Child*: Linda / Linda's son / Emeka / Emeka's father

4 *The House*: Sonny / Nan

5 *The Deceivers*: Gbenga / Mervyn

6 *Callus*: the wife / the husband

7 *Chinna and Muthu*: Chinna / Chinna's father / the goat

8 *The Festive Season in a Part of Africa*: the vet / Granny / Mbambo

I felt	afraid for angry with pleased with sorry for	———	when because	———

3 Use the clues to complete the crossword with words from the stories (one word from each story). All words go across.

1 Nan in Jamaica agreed about the house because she _____ Sonny.

2 Gbenga made a new friend online in a _____ room.

3 The cow in South Africa had a _____ waiting to be born.

4 In Chinna's village people believed that the Rain Gods needed a _____.

5 Linda wanted Emeka's family to _____ him.

6 Leonard's wife _____ him a scarf which was full of holes.

7 The Chinese wife wanted to talk about her _____, but her husband did not want to hear.

8 The _____ inside the American teenager is not for food.

4 Find the hidden word (8 letters) in the completed crossword above. Which story does it come from? What does it mean?

1 The word is _____, from the story _____.

2 The word means _____.

5 In *The Festive Season in a Part of Africa,* why did the vet say that half of 2,000 rands was 750, not 1,000? Look at these two ideas, and decide which one is best for the story.

   1 He made a mistake because he was not good at numbers.
   2 He did not really make a mistake; he wanted to give
      Granny a good price because it was the festive season.

6 Here is a short poem (a kind of poem called a haiku) about one of the stories. Which of the eight stories is it about?

> *The face of hunger.*
> *Just a pretty photograph*
> *in a magazine.*

Here is another haiku. Which story is this one about?

> *Don't try to meet them.*
> *Don't go there. Don't ask questions.*
> *Better not to know.*

A haiku is a Japanese poem, which is always in three lines, and the three lines always have 5, 7, and 5 syllables each, like this:

| The | face | of | hun | ger | = 5 syllables
| Just | a | pret | ty | pho | to | graph | = 7 syllables
| in | a | mag | az | ine? | = 5 syllables

Now write your own haiku, one for each of the other six stories. Think about what each story is really about. What are the important ideas for you? Remember to keep to three lines of 5, 7, 5 syllables each.

ABOUT THE AUTHORS

SEFI ATTA

Sefi Atta (1964–) was born in Lagos, Nigeria. She was educated in Nigeria, England, and the United States, and worked for many years as a qualified accountant. She lives in Mississippi, USA, with her husband and daughter, and teaches at a university. Her short stories have won several awards, and she has written plays for the radio and the theatre. Her first novel, *Everything Good Will Come*, was published in 2005, and in 2006 it won the first Wole Soyinka Prize for Literature in Africa.

ADRIENNE M. FRATER

Adrienne Frater lives and writes in Nelson, New Zealand. She was a teacher for many years, but is now a full-time writer, writing stories for both adults and children. She loves to travel, and writes anywhere – on boats or in a motorhome. The idea for her story *Leonard* came to her like this. Her friend's son made a beautiful wooden box for his mother, out of old wood, but the wood was thin and had holes in it. It was a present full of holes, but made with great love, like the scarf in the story.

ANTHONY C. DIALA

Anthony Diala, a Nigerian, is a human rights lawyer and a university teacher. He has worked in several international organizations, notably the Hague-based International Criminal Court. A one-time newspaper columnist, he writes as a hobby, and his manuscripts include novels, short stories, and a play. The idea for *The Strange Child* came from a story from his own village in south-east Nigeria. The story centred on a man who, people said, died in a car accident – but continued living in the city until a relative found him, and then he disappeared.

ERICA N. ROBINSON

Erica Robinson-Sturridge was born in the town of Mandeville in Jamaica, where she spent her early years. As a child, she loved reading and writing, and playing on the beach, and she continued to read literature while she was studying at university for her degrees in Biology and Nutrition. She still works as a scientist, but hopes one day to be a full-time writer. She lives with her husband in her hometown in Jamaica.

FOLAKEMI EMEM-AKPAN

Folakemi Emem-Akpan lives in Lagos, Nigeria, with her family. She works as a financial journalist but feels more comfortable thinking of herself as a writer. She has written stories since she was five years old, encouraged by her mother, aunts, and friends. Her first book, *Touch My Pain*, was published in 2004. She hopes one day to stop her day job, and become a writer full-time.

JANET TAY HUI CHING

Janet Tay Hui Ching (1976–) was born in Malaysia, and was educated in Sarawak and at university in England. She worked as an advocate and solicitor for five years in Kuala Lumpur, Malaysia, before leaving the legal profession to become an editor at a local publishing house. The idea for her story *Callus* came to her while listening to stories told at a family party for her grandmother's birthday.

SUCHITRA KARTHIK KUMAR

Suchitra Karthik Kumar is a radio broadcaster who hosts the daily live breakfast show on Hello FM in Chennai, India. She is also a professional singer and travels the world, giving singing performances. Two of her short stories have been Highly Commended by the Commonwealth Broadcasting Association: *The Runaway Peppercorn* in the 2003 competition, and *Chinna and Muthu* in the 2005 competition. She lives in a tiny apartment by the sea, with her actor husband Karthik and their little dog, Kapalee.

TOD COLLINS

Tod Collins is a South African whose family came to Natal in the mid-1850s. As a child he lived on a farm, and later studied veterinary science, becoming a qualified vet in 1973. He now lives in a small mountain village, where he works as a vet and climbs mountains in his spare time. He is not a professional writer, he says. He writes mostly to keep a record for his family, but he enjoys describing his adventures as a country vet and his experiences in the mountains of KwaZulu-Natal and Lesotho.

OXFORD BOOKWORMS LIBRARY

Classics • Crime & Mystery • Factfiles • Fantasy & Horror
Human Interest • Playscripts • Thriller & Adventure
True Stories • World Stories

The OXFORD BOOKWORMS LIBRARY provides enjoyable reading in English, with a wide range of classic and modern fiction, non-fiction, and plays. It includes original and adapted texts in seven carefully graded language stages, which take learners from beginner to advanced level. An overview is given on the next pages.

All Stage 1 titles are available as audio recordings, as well as over eighty other titles from Starter to Stage 6. All Starters and many titles at Stages 1 to 4 are specially recommended for younger learners. Every Bookworm is illustrated, and Starters and Factfiles have full-colour illustrations.

The OXFORD BOOKWORMS LIBRARY also offers extensive support. Each book contains an introduction to the story, notes about the author, a glossary, and activities. Additional resources include tests and worksheets, and answers for these and for the activities in the books. There is advice on running a class library, using audio recordings, and the many ways of using Oxford Bookworms in reading programmes. Resource materials are available on the website <www.oup.com/elt/gradedreaders>.

You can find details and a full list of titles in the *Oxford Bookworms Library Catalogue* and *Oxford English Language Teaching Catalogues*, and on the website <www.oup.com/elt/gradedreaders>.

THE OXFORD BOOKWORMS LIBRARY GRADING AND SAMPLE EXTRACTS

STARTER • 250 HEADWORDS

present simple – present continuous – imperative –
can/cannot, must – *going to* (future) – simple gerunds ...

Her phone is ringing – but where is it?

Sally gets out of bed and looks in her bag. No phone. She looks under the bed. No phone. Then she looks behind the door. There is her phone. Sally picks up her phone and answers it. *Sally's Phone*

STAGE 1 • 400 HEADWORDS

... past simple – coordination with *and, but, or* –
subordination with *before, after, when, because, so* ...

I knew him in Persia. He was a famous builder and I worked with him there. For a time I was his friend, but not for long. When he came to Paris, I came after him – I wanted to watch him. He was a very clever, very dangerous man. *The Phantom of the Opera*

STAGE 2 • 700 HEADWORDS

... present perfect – *will* (future) – *(don't) have to, must not, could* –
comparison of adjectives – simple *if* clauses – past continuous –
tag questions – *ask/tell* + infinitive ...

While I was writing these words in my diary, I decided what to do. I must try to escape. I shall try to get down the wall outside. The window is high above the ground, but I have to try. I shall take some of the gold with me – if I escape, perhaps it will be helpful later. *Dracula*

STAGE 3 • 1000 HEADWORDS

... should, may – present perfect continuous – *used to* – past perfect –
causative – relative clauses – indirect statements ...

Of course, it was most important that no one should see
Colin, Mary, or Dickon entering the secret garden. So Colin
gave orders to the gardeners that they must all keep away
from that part of the garden in future. *The Secret Garden*

STAGE 4 • 1400 HEADWORDS

... past perfect continuous – passive (simple forms) –
would conditional clauses – indirect questions –
relatives with *where/when* – gerunds after prepositions/phrases ...

I was glad. Now Hyde could not show his face to the world
again. If he did, every honest man in London would be
proud to report him to the police. *Dr Jekyll and Mr Hyde*

STAGE 5 • 1800 HEADWORDS

... future continuous – future perfect –
passive (modals, continuous forms) –
would have conditional clauses – modals + perfect infinitive ...

If he had spoken Estella's name, I would have hit him. I was so
angry with him, and so depressed about my future, that I could
not eat the breakfast. Instead I went straight to the old house.
Great Expectations

STAGE 6 • 2500 HEADWORDS

... passive (infinitives, gerunds) – advanced modal meanings –
clauses of concession, condition

When I stepped up to the piano, I was confident. It was as if I
knew that the prodigy side of me really did exist. And when I
started to play, I was so caught up in how lovely I looked that
I didn't worry how I would sound. *The Joy Luck Club*

WORLD STORIES FROM BOOKWORMS

The Meaning of Gifts: Stories from Turkey
STAGE 1 · RETOLD BY JENNIFER BASSETT

Stories from the Heart: Stories from Around the World
STAGE 2 · RETOLD BY JENNIFER BASSETT

Changing their Skies: Stories from Africa
STAGE 2 · RETOLD BY JENNIFER BASSETT

The Long White Cloud: Stories from New Zealand
STAGE 3 · RETOLD BY CHRISTINE LINDOP

Playing with Fire: Stories from the Pacific Rim *
STAGE 3 · RETOLD BY JENNIFER BASSETT

A Cup of Kindness: Stories from Scotland
STAGE 3 · RETOLD BY JENNIFER BASSETT

Land of my Childhood: Stories from South Asia **
STAGE 4 · RETOLD BY CLARE WEST

The Price of Peace: Stories from Africa
STAGE 4 · RETOLD BY CHRISTINE LINDOP

A Time of Waiting: Stories from Around the World
STAGE 4 · RETOLD BY CLARE WEST

** Winner: Language Learner Literature Awards
* Finalist: Language Learner Literature Awards